SUPERSTARS OF WRESTLING

JOHN CENA

By Ryan Nagelhout

Gareth Stevens
Publishing

Please visit our website, www.garethstevens.com. For a free color catalog of all our high-quality books, call toll free 1-800-542-2595 or fax 1-877-542-2596.

Library of Congress Cataloging-in-Publication Data

Nagelhout, Ryan.
 John Cena / Ryan Nagelhout.
     p. cm. — (Superstars of wrestling)
 Includes index.
ISBN 978-1-4339-8528-7 (pbk.)
ISBN 978-1-4339-8529-4 (6-pack)
ISBN 978-1-4339-8527-0 (library binding)
1. Cena, John—Juvenile literature. 2. Wrestlers—United States—Biography—Juvenile
literature. I. Title.
GV1196.C46N34 2013
796.812092—dc23
 [B]
                                    2012029064

First Edition

Published in 2013 by Gareth Stevens Publishing
111 East 14th Street, Suite 349
New York, NY 10003

Copyright © 2013 Gareth Stevens Publishing

Designer: Nicholas Domiano
Editor: Ryan Nagelhout

Photo credits: Cover background Shutterstock.com; cover, p. 1 KMazur/WireImage/Getty
Images; p. 5, 17 Ethan Miller/Getty Images Entertainment/Getty Images; p. 7 Ron Elkman/
Getty Images Sport/Getty Images; p. 9 Moses Robinson/ Getty Images Entertainment/
Getty Images; p. 11 Rick Scuteri/AP Photo; p. 13 Don Arnold/WireImage/Getty Images;
p. 15 Denise Truscello/WireImage/Getty Images; p. 19, 27 Ray Tamarra/ Getty Images
Entertainment/Getty Images; p. 21 Juli Hansen/Shutterstock.com; p. 23 George Napolitano/
FilmMagic/Getty Images; p . 25 TIZIANA FABI/AFP/Getty Images; p. 29 Andrew H.
Walker/Getty Images Entertainment/Getty Images;

Printed in the United States of America

CPSIA compliance information: Batch #CW13GS: For further information contact Gareth Stevens, New York, New York at 1-800-542-2595.

Contents

Meet Cena

John Cena is a WWE superstar!

5

Cena was born on April 23, 1977. He grew up in West Newbury, Massachusetts. His dad works as a wrestling announcer.

7

Cena went to college to play football.

He was a Division III All-American.

He graduated in 1998.

9

Going "Pro"

In 2000, Cena started wrestling in California. His ring name was The Prototype.

In 2001, Cena signed with the WWE. He moved to Ohio Valley Wrestling with future stars like Chris Jericho and Brock Lesnar.

Big Time

In 2002, Cena made his WWE debut against Kurt Angle. Despite a tough loss, he won fans over right away.

First Title

Cena's first title came in 2004 when he won the United States Championship. The next year, he won the WWE Championship at WrestleMania 21!

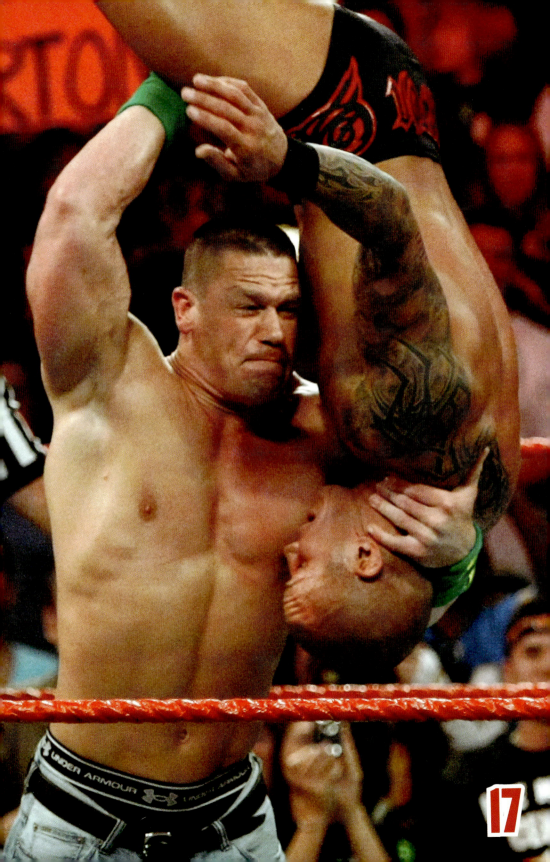

17

Making Music

Cena loves hip-hop music. In 2005, he released his own album, *You Can't See Me*. The album's name became his trademark.

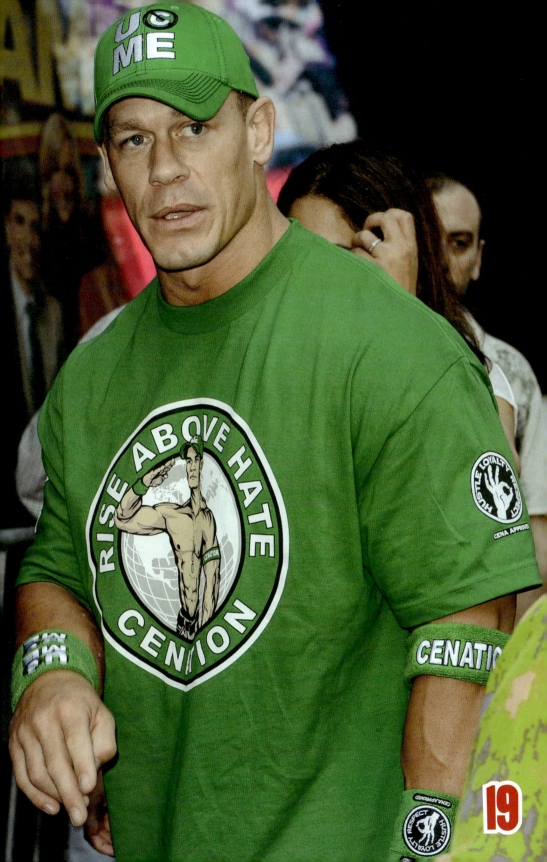

19

The Big Screen

Cena has also taken Hollywood by storm. In 2006, he starred as John Triton in *The Marine*. He's also played Fred's dad in the *Fred* movies.

The titles kept on coming for Cena. In 2008, he won the WWE World Heavyweight Championship.

23

The Champ

Cena has won the WWE title so many times that he goes by the nickname "The Champ."

Giving Grappler

Cena loves to give back to his fans.

He's a big part of WWE's Be a STAR

antibullying campaign.

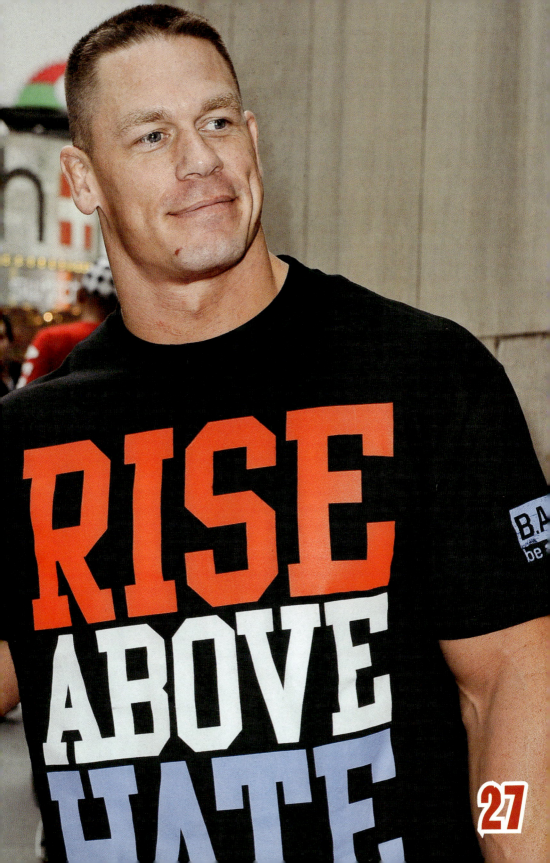

27

He also works with the Make-A-Wish Foundation. Since 2004, he has made over 300 wishes come true!

Timeline

1977   John Cena is born on April 23.

2000   Cena starts wrestling in California.

2002   Cena makes his WWE debut.

2004   Cena wins first title, the United States Championship.

2005   Cena wins WWE Championship at WrestleMania 21.

Cena releases his album *You Can't See Me*.

2006   Cena stars in the film *The Marine*.

2008   Cena wins World Heavyweight Championship.

For More Information

Books:

O'Shei, Tim. *John Cena*. Mankato, MN: Capstone Press, 2010.

Shields, Brian. *John Cena*. New York, NY: DK Publishing, 2009.

Websites:

J-Cena.com

www.j-cena.com
This fan site is the ultimate source for John Cena news.

John Cena's Wrestling Profile

www.onlineworldofwrestling.com/profiles/j/john-cena.html
See results from Cena's matches at his Online World of Wrestling page.

Glossary

announcer: a person whose job is to describe a sports event as it happens

division: a unit or part of a bigger group

Hollywood: a part of Los Angeles, California, where many movies are made

prototype: the original model on which something is made

trademark: something that identifies a person or thing

Index